Arrow Book of Good 'n' Easy Cooking

by SANDRA SANDERS

illustrated by Mike Quon

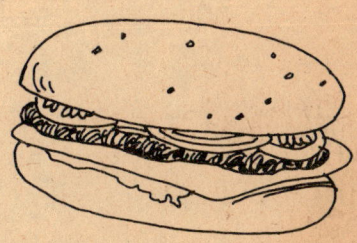

SCHOLASTIC BOOK SERVICES
New York Toronto London Sydney Auckland Tokyo

To my mother

No part of this publication may be reproduced in whole or in part, or stored in a retrieval system, or transmitted in any form or by any means, electronic, mechanical, photocopying, recording, or otherwise, without written permission of the publisher. For information regarding permission, write to Scholastic Book Services, 50 West 44th Street, New York, NY 10036.

ISBN 0-590-30066-0

Copyright © 1979 by Scholastic Magazines, Inc. All rights reserved. Published by Scholastic Book Services, a division of Scholastic Magazines, Inc.

12 11 10 9 8 7 6 5 4 3 2 1   11   9/7 0 1 2 3 4/8

Printed in the U. S. A.   07

COOKING is fun, and it's easy when you follow the recipes in this book. You can turn out heavenly hamburgers, perfect pizzas, chicken delights, or yummy desserts in your own kitchen, for your family and your friends. You can make your favorite breakfast or lunch, or whip up a treat for the family dinner, or cook the entire meal.

The secret of serving any meal is *planning*. Read through the recipes the day before you want to cook. Decide what you will make. Mix and match the recipes any way you like, or follow the menus given in the book.

Once you've decided what you'll make, check to see if you have all the ingredients and cooking equipment you will need.

Give yourself plenty of time (at least an hour) to prepare the meal. If you plan to serve a dessert, it's better to make it first, before you start preparing the main course.

And before you cook, be sure to read through the safety and cooking tips at the back of the book. *Bon appétit!*

Contents

Breakfast

Menus and Place Setting	6-7
Fresh-Squeezed Orange Juice	8
Breakfast Cocktails	9
Orange Blossom Float	9
Snowy Orange and Banana Slices	10
Summer Berries	11
Quick Cinnamon Toast	12
Cinnamon Toast in the Oven	12
French Toast	13
Hard-Boiled Eggs	14
Scrambled Egg Omelet	15
Pancakes	16
Bacon	17

Lunch

Menus for Home and for School	18-19
Hamburgers	20
Cheeseburgers	22
Pizzas	23
Super Sandwiches	24
Super Heroes	25
Lime and Ginger Salad	26
Waldorf Salad	28
Peanut Butter Bread	29

Dinner

Menus	30-31
Meat Loaf with Tangy Sauce	32
Individual Meat Loaves	34
Crunchy Baked Chicken	35
Spaghetti with Meat Sauce	36
Frankfurters	
with Cheese or Bacon	38
with Mustard, Relish, or Sauerkraut	39
In-a-Blanket	39
Baked Potatoes	40
Mixed Green Salad	41
Candied Carrots	42

Desserts and Party Treats

Chocolate Cupcakes	44	Ribbon Sandwiches	55
Creamy White Frosting	46	Pinwheels	56
Ice Cream	47	Celery Logs	57
Refrigerator Cookies	48-49	Stuffed Eggs	57
Apple Crunch	50	Lemonade	58
Apple Sauce	51	Sparkling Cranberry Punch	59
Chocolate Cookie Roll	52		
Cocoa	54	Pink Lemonade	59

Safety Tips and Cooking Tips   60-61

Cooking Equipment (names and pictures)   62-63

Breakfast

Menus

French Toast
Snowy Orange and Banana Slices
Cocoa

Orange Juice
Cinnamon Toast
Scrambled Eggs
Milk

Tomato Juice
Scrambled Egg Omelet
Plain Toast with Jelly
Milk

Cranberry Cocktail
Bacon Sandwich on Plain Toast
Cocoa

Orange Juice
Hard-Boiled Egg
Quick Cinnamon Toast
Milk

Pineapple Cocktail
Pancakes
Bacon
Milk

Before you start to cook, set the table with the dishes, silverware, napkins — and whatever else you'll need — for a tempting breakfast.

Fresh-Squeezed Orange Juice

Canned, frozen, or pasteurized orange juice is quicker if you're making breakfast for the whole family. But nothing tastes as good as the wake-up flavor of fresh-squeezed orange juice.

Use one large orange for each person. Cut the orange in half around the smooth middle — not through the pitted ends. Squeeze half the orange and remove the pits from the squeezer with a spoon. Pour the juice — pulp and all — into a small glass. Then squeeze the other half of the orange.

Breakfast Cocktails

Ready-to-serve cranberry, or grapefruit, or pineapple juices make good breakfast drinks. Serve them plain or mixed with fresh orange juice. Use 1 part ready-to-serve juice with 1 part fresh orange juice.

If you sometimes want a breakfast drink that isn't sweet, try a glass of canned tomato juice and stir in the juice of a quarter of a lemon. It is delicious with a scrambled egg omelet or a bacon sandwich in the morning.

Orange Blossom Float

In a small bowl, mash a small, ripe banana with a fork. Add the juice of 2 oranges. Beat with an eggbeater until the banana is smooth. Pour into a tall glass.

Snowy Orange and Banana Slices

This recipe makes enough for 2 servings. You can put half of it in a small plastic container and take it to school for lunch.

1 orange
1 ripe banana
shredded coconut

The night before you serve this, peel the orange. Clean off as much of the white skin as you can. Separate the orange into sections, and put it in a covered bowl in the refrigerator.

Next morning, cut a small ripe banana into the bowl with the orange sections. Mix gently, then spoon into a dessert dish. Sprinkle shredded coconut over the fruit just before you serve it.

This recipe also makes a delicious dessert for dinner.

Summer Berries

Berries are a good early summer breakfast, lunch, or dinner treat.

Blueberries: Use about 2 or 3 handfuls of berries per serving. Put the berries in a strainer or colander and wash thoroughly under running water. Pick out any bad berries. Let drain, then serve with milk or cream and a little sugar. Or add a handful of berries to your favorite dry cereal.

Strawberries: Use about 8 or 10 medium-sized berries per serving. Pick off the green stems. Wash the berries in a strainer or colander under running water. Drain, then cut each berry in half. Serve with milk or cream and a little sugar. Or add to your favorite cereal.

Quick Cinnamon Toast

1 tablespoon granulated sugar
1 teaspoon cinnamon

Mix the sugar and cinnamon in a cup.

Next, make **plain toast**: Set the toaster at medium and butter the toast generously as soon as it pops from the toaster.

With a spoon, shake the sugar and cinnamon over the toast. Serve while hot. It's delicious with fresh fruit.

Cinnamon Toast in the Oven

3 tablespoons softened butter or margarine
5 tablespoons granulated sugar
1½ teaspoons cinnamon
6 slices bread

Set the oven at 400°. Have an ungreased cookie sheet ready. Mix the butter, sugar, and cinnamon in a small bowl. With a knife, spread the mixture on one side of each slice of bread. Put the bread on the cookie sheet. Toast in the oven for 8 minutes.

For variety: Use maple sugar or brown sugar instead of cinnamon.

French Toast

2 eggs
½ cup milk
¼ teaspoon salt
¼ teaspoon vanilla extract
4 slices white bread

1. In a wide, flat bowl, beat the eggs, milk, salt, and vanilla with a fork until well mixed.
2. Put 2 tablespoons of butter or margarine in a frying pan. Turn the heat to low. Melt the butter or margarine.
3. Lay a piece of bread in the egg mixture and let it soak on both sides.
4. Turn the heat to medium.
5. With a pancake turner, lift the bread and lay it in the frying pan.
6. When the toast is browned on one side, turn it over. If the pan becomes dry while you are cooking, add more butter or margarine.
7. Put the toast on a platter in the oven until all the slices are ready.
8. Serve with honey or maple syrup.

French toast makes a delicious weekend family breakfast treat.

Hard-Boiled Eggs

1. Put the unshelled egg in a saucepan and cover with cold water. If you use an egg right out of the refrigerator, add a tablespoon of salt and a few drops of vinegar to the water. This will help to keep the egg from cracking.
2. Place the pan over medium heat and bring to a boil. Turn the heat down, until the water is just simmering, and cook the egg for 15 minutes.
3. Then put the pan under the cold water faucet and let the water run into the pan until it's full of cold water. This will stop the egg from cooking, and keep a dark ring from forming around the yolk.
4. *To shell hard-boiled eggs:* When shell is cool enough to handle, tap the egg lightly against a hard surface and roll it between your hands until the shell is shattered all around. Then peel off the shell.
5. Cut the egg up in an egg cup and eat it with salt and butter.

   Note: If you want to eat or use it cold later on, let the egg cool and put it, *unshelled*, into the refrigerator.

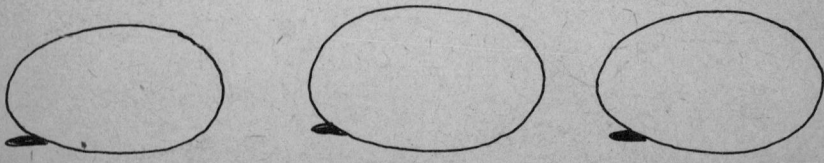

Scrambled Egg Omelet

2 eggs
2 tablespoons milk
¼ teaspoon salt
sprinkle of pepper

1. Break the eggs into a bowl. Add the milk, salt, and pepper. Beat with an eggbeater or fork.
2. Turn the heat to medium and melt 2 tablespoons of butter or margarine in a frying pan. Pour in the eggs.
3. As soon as the eggs begin to harden around the edges, use a fork to pull back the edges and let the soft egg from the center flow out to the sides of the pan. Tip the pan slightly.
4. When all the egg is cooked, fold the omelet in half with a pancake turner.
5. Remove from the pan and serve hot.

For variety: Before you fold the omelet, you can sprinkle bits of cheese or crumbled bacon over the egg. Of course, you can also make regular scrambled eggs by stirring the eggs in the pan as they are cooking.

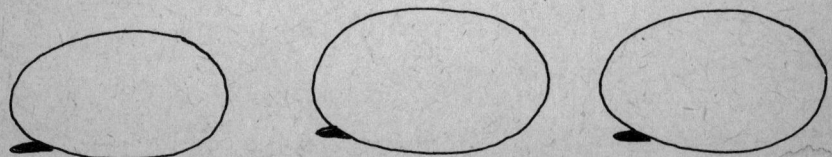

Pancakes

Makes about 10 3-inch pancakes.

⅔ cup flour
1 teaspoon baking powder
1 teaspoon baking soda
1 teaspoon sugar
¼ teaspoon salt
1 egg, beaten
⅔ cup milk (mix into it 1 teaspoon vinegar)
2 tablespoons cooking oil

1. Sift all the dry ingredients into a large bowl.
2. Combine the egg, milk, and cooking oil in another bowl, and add them to the flour mixture.
3. Blend gently by rotating the spoon so that you fold the flour into the egg mixture. *Do not beat.* Mixture will be thin and lumpy. Let the batter stand.
4. Heat the oven to 170° and put a platter in to warm.
5. Grease a griddle by wiping some cooking oil over it. Heat griddle to medium and test by drops of water. When the water sizzles and bounces, but doesn't disappear in steam, the griddle is just right.
6. Stir the batter once and drop by tablespoons onto the griddle. One tablespoon makes a 3-inch cake. Cook on one side for about 2 minutes or until the cakes show bubbles and look dry along the edge.
7. Flip the cakes over with a pancake turner and cook about 1–2 minutes on the other side.

8. As soon as you finish making a batch, flip the pancakes onto the platter in the oven.
9. Serve with butter, maple syrup, and bacon.

Bacon

1. Put 2 slices of bacon into a dry frying pan. Turn the heat to medium.
2. Fry until the bacon begins to curl and the edges turn brown.
3. Turn the slices over with a fork. Continue to fry until the bacon is done the way you like it — chewy or crisp.
4. Put a paper towel on a plate.
5. Remove the bacon from the pan with a fork or tongs and place it on the paper towel to drain off the grease.

    A bacon sandwich, on plain bread or toast, makes a nice change for breakfast.

Lunch

Menus for Home

Pizzas
Waldorf Salad
Refrigerator Cookies
Lemonade

Frankfurter-on-a-Roll
Waldorf Salad
Lemonade

Hamburger
Lime and Ginger Salad
Refrigerator Cookies
Milk

Hero Sandwich
Frosted Chocolate Cupcake
Milk

Menus for School

Tuna Fish Salad on a Roll
Celery Hearts
Frosted Chocolate Cupcake
Milk

Peanut Butter and Banana on Peanut Butter Bread
Carrot Strips
Refrigerator Cookies
Milk

Cream Cheese and Marmalade on
Date-and-Nut Bread
Apple, Grapes, or Pear
Milk

Meat Loaf with Ketchup
Raw Green Pepper Slices
Snowy Orange and Banana Slices
Milk

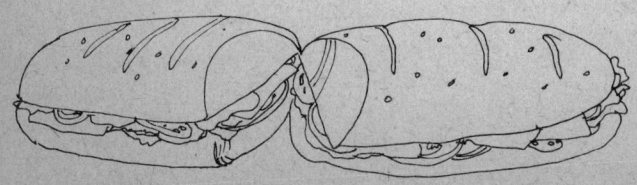

Hamburgers

¾ pound of ground beef (chuck)

This will make 4 hamburger patties. If you buy the meat the day before you want to serve it, you can make the patties ahead of time. Wrap each one separately in wax paper. Put them in the freezer until you are ready to use them. Take them out of the freezer 4 or 5 hours before you want to cook them—just before you go to school. Let them thaw in the wrapping in the refrigerator.

---

1. With your hands, scoop up enough meat to make one patty. Shape it in your hands, lightly.
2. Line the bottom of the broiler pan with a piece of aluminum foil. This will catch the drippings and make it easier to clean up.
3. Then lightly grease the broiler rack, and place it about 4 inches from the heat.
4. Turn on the broiler and let the rack heat up for a minute or two.
5. Carefully place the patties on the rack and let them cook for 3 minutes.
6. Turn them over with a spatula. For:
    rare hamburgers, cook for another 5 minutes,
    for medium, 9 minutes,
    for well done, 11 minutes.

While you're waiting, warm the hamburger rolls in the oven or in the toaster. When the hamburgers are ready, sprinkle them with salt and pepper and add anything else you like — lettuce, sliced tomatoes or onion, pickles, mustard, ketchup, mayonnaise — or all of them!

Cheeseburgers

Shape ground meat into hamburgers and either broil them (see page 20) or fry them. If you broil them, put a slice of cheese on each patty 2 minutes before removing them from the broiler.

If you fry them:

1. Put a greased frying pan over medium heat.
2. After a minute place the patties in the pan and brown on one side.
3. Turn them over with a turner and put a slice of American cheese on top of each.
4. While the second side browns, heat hamburger rolls in the oven (250°).
5. To help melt the cheese, cover the pan with a lid for a couple of minutes.
6. Remove the rolls from the oven, open them, and put a patty inside.

Cheeseburgers taste even better with a slice of tomato on top of the cheese.

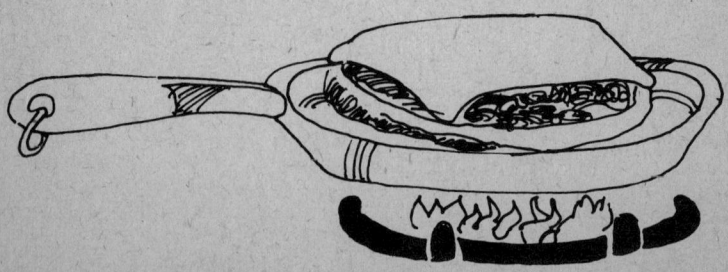

Pizzas

2 English muffins
6-ounce can tomato paste or
1 can pizza sauce
¼ teaspoon oregano
package of shredded mozzarella cheese

1. Heat the oven to 400°. Have an ungreased cookie sheet ready.
2. With a fork, separate the muffin in half.
3. Mix the tomato paste and oregano in a small bowl.
4. Spread the soft side of each muffin half with a thin layer of the tomato mixture.
5. Sprinkle the cheese over the top.
6. Put the muffins on the cookie sheet. Bake for 10 minutes. Serve hot.

For variety: Put small pieces of salami, pepperoni, or ham on top of the cheese before you put the pizzas in the oven.

Super Sandwiches

If you take your lunch to school, or eat at home, you can make super sandwich fillings — a different one for each day of the week.

Fix carrot strips, celery hearts, raw green pepper slices, or radishes to munch along with your sandwiches.

These fillings are good on any kind of bread — white, pumpernickel, rolls, date-and-nut bread — or your own peanut butter bread. (To make it, see recipe on page 29.)

Peanut butter with
- *sliced banana
- *chopped celery
- *chopped apple
- *raisins and honey
- *chopped bacon
- *apricot jam

Cream Cheese with
- *chopped walnuts
- *chopped olives
- *orange marmalade
- *chopped radishes, carrots, and green pepper

Tuna Fish or **Hard-Boiled Egg** with
- *chopped celery, chopped onions, chopped sweet pickle — all mixed together with mayonnaise

Your own Meat Loaf with
- *mustard or ketchup (See page 32 for meat loaf recipe.)

Super Heroes

1. Cut a small loaf of French or Italian bread in half. Then cut each half the long way.
2. On one side of each half loaf, put some or all of these fillers:

    Slices of salami, ham, or bologna
    Lettuce; tomato slices; pickles
    Slices of American or Swiss cheese

3. Put the remaining halves of the loaf on top and serve.

Lime and Ginger Salad

for salad or dessert

1 cup water
1 package lime gelatin
20-ounce can pineapple chunks or sliced peaches, drained

½ cup juice from drained pineapple or peaches
½ cup ginger ale

1. Boil the water in a small saucepan. Remove from the heat.
2. Shake the lime gelatin over the water and stir until dissolved.
3. Add the canned fruit juice, ginger ale, and the canned fruit. Stir gently.
4. Pour into a jelly mold or a bowl or into 4 individual dessert glasses. Chill in the refrigerator for 2 hours.
5. *To remove gelatin from mold:* Fill a wide bowl with hot water. Dip just the bottom half of the mold into the water for a second. Don't let any water get on the gelatin. Hold a flat dinner plate over the top of the mold and turn the mold and the plate, together, upside down.

Serving the Lime and Ginger Salad

You can serve the mold as a family or a party dessert. Decorate the plate with a ring of refrigerator cookies (for recipe see page 48), and spoon the salad into dessert dishes.

You can also serve it as a real salad. Decorate the mold with a ring of lettuce and cut portions of the mold at the table. Put a lettuce leaf on each salad plate, lay a slice of the salad mold on it, and serve with mayonnaise or a mixture of mayonnaise and unsweetened whipped cream.

If you jelled the salad in individual dessert glasses, serve them with a dab of whipped cream or vanilla ice cream on top.

Waldorf Salad

2 red apples
½ cup chopped walnuts
3 stalks celery
small head iceberg lettuce

This delicious recipe makes enough for 4 people.

1. Peel off 2 or 3 large leaves of lettuce for each person.
2. Wash and dry the leaves, then arrange them on individual salad plates. Store the rest of the unwashed lettuce in the refrigerator.
3. Wash the apples well and cut in quarters to remove the cores. Then cut up into small pieces, but don't peel the apples.
4. Wash the celery and cut up into small pieces.
5. Mix the apples, celery, and walnuts together in a bowl.
6. Spoon the apple mixture onto the lettuce leaves.
7. Top with your favorite salad dressing. Mayonnaise is most popular with Waldorf salad.

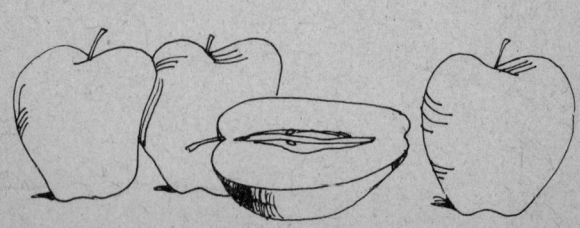

Peanut Butter Bread

- 2 cups all-purpose flour
- 4 teaspoons baking powder
- 1 teaspoon salt
- ⅓ cup granulated sugar
- ½ cup peanut butter
- 1½ cups milk

1. Heat the oven to 350°.
2. Grease a loaf pan.
3. Sift the flour, baking powder, salt, and sugar into a large bowl.
4. Add the peanut butter and mix with a fork until the batter is crumbly.
5. Add the milk and mix thoroughly with a spoon.
6. Pour the batter into the pan.
7. Bake for 1 hour.
8. Let the bread cool in the pan before removing it to a cake rack.

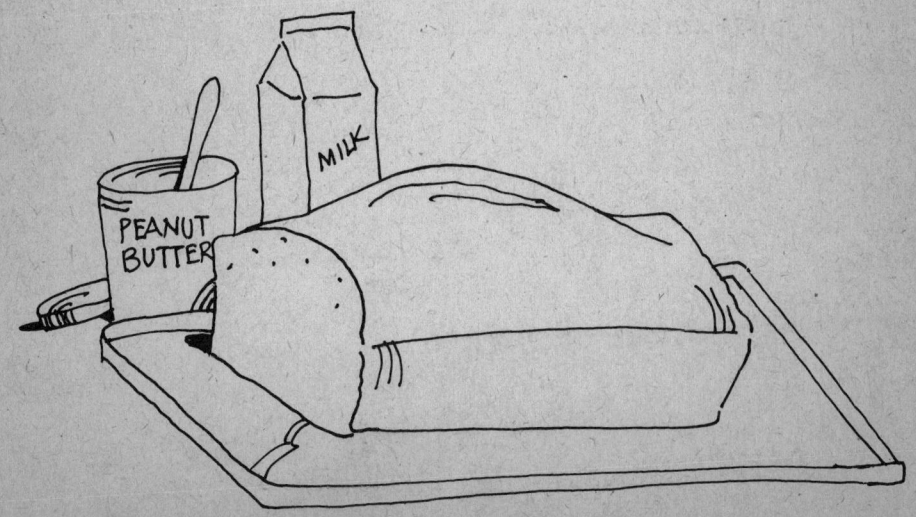

Dinner

Menus

Spaghetti
Mixed Green Salad
Ice Cream and Cookies
Lemonade

Omelet with Cheese
Waldorf Salad
Refrigerator Cookies
Cocoa

Crunchy Chicken
Candied Carrots
Waldorf Salad
Strawberries and Cream
Milk

Menus

Franks-in-a-Blanket
Candied Carrots
Lime and Ginger Salad
Lemonade

Meat Loaf
Baked Potato
Mixed Green Salad
Frosted Chocolate Cupcake
Milk

Franks-and-Bacon
Mixed Green Salad
Apple Crunch
Milk

Meat Loaf with Tangy Sauce

¾ cup dry bread crumbs
¾ cup milk or tomato juice or bouillon
1 egg, beaten
1 small, chopped onion
1 teaspoon salt
½ teaspoon pepper
1½ pounds lean ground beef

1. Grease a loaf pan.
2. Put the bread crumbs and the milk (or tomato juice or bouillon) in a large bowl. Let the bread crumbs soak until they are completely wet.
3. Add the beaten egg, chopped onion, salt, and pepper. Mix well.
4. Add the ground beef.
5. With clean hands, work the ingredients together until they are well mixed.

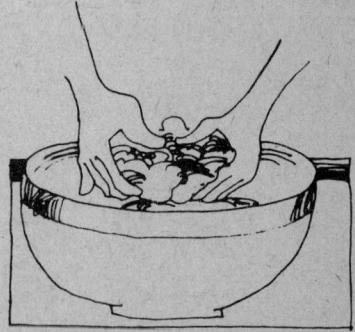

6. In the bowl, shape the mixture into a firm ball.
7. Move the ball to a workboard, and shape it into a loaf a little narrower than the loaf pan. Use flattened hands to mold the sides. Pat the top smooth.
8. With a spatula underneath it, lift the meat loaf into the loaf pan. Press closed any cracks. Loaf should not touch the pan's sides.
9. Heat the oven to 350°.
10. *For topping, mix together*:
    ¼ cup ketchup
    3 tablespoons brown sugar
    2 teaspoons mustard
    and spread the mixture over the meat.
11. Bake the meat loaf for 1 hour. Serve with a salad and baked potatoes (see page 40).

Individual Meat Loaves

You can also make small, individual meat loaves for each member of the family, using the meat loaf recipe on the preceding page.

1st method: Shape the mixture into large, plump, round hamburgers, one for each person. Put them on a flat greased pan or on a pan lined with aluminum foil and spoon the topping over each cake. Bake for 25 minutes at 350°.

2nd method: Fill greased muffin tins ⅔ full of meat loaf mixture. (Make two cakes for each person.) Top with a little of the ketchup mixture. Bake for 15 minutes at 350°.

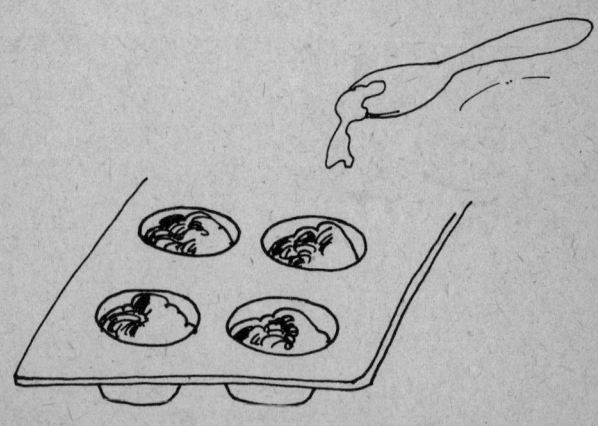

Crunchy Baked Chicken

8 pieces of chicken (drumsticks, wings, breasts, whatever is your favorite)

¼ cup flour, unsifted
1 teaspoon salt
1 teaspoon paprika
⅛ teaspoon pepper

1. Wash and dry the chicken pieces with a paper towel.
2. Heat the oven to 350°.
3. Grease a large baking pan.
4. Put the flour, salt, paprika, and pepper in a paper bag. Hold the top of the bag tightly closed and shake until the flour and seasonings are well mixed.
5. Put 2 or 3 pieces of chicken in the bag at a time. Close the bag tightly again, and shake until the pieces of chicken are well coated.
6. Bake for 1 hour. (You can bake potatoes at the same time. See page 40.)
7. Serve on a warm platter decorated with parsley.

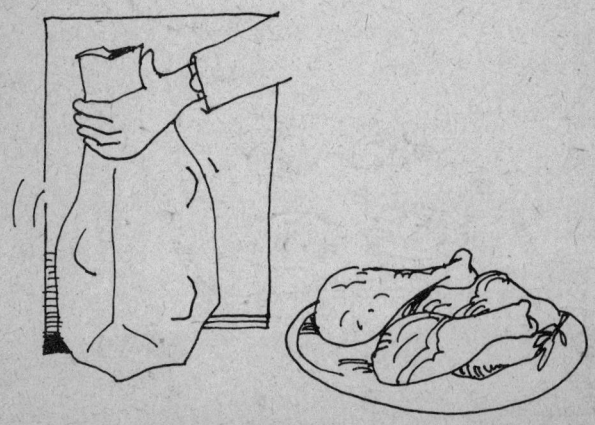

Spaghetti with Meat Sauce

The Sauce

You can make this a day ahead, or the afternoon of the day you want to serve it. It takes from 1 to 3 hours to cook and serves 4 people.

½ pound ground beef
2 medium-sized onions
16-ounce can whole, peeled tomatoes
6-ounce can tomato paste
1 teaspoon salt
1 teaspoon oregano

1. Mix the tomatoes (use the juice too), tomato paste, salt, and oregano in a large bowl.
2. Peel and cut up the onions on a board. (See Safety Tips 6 and 7, page 60.)
3. Heat about a tablespoon of vegetable oil in a large frying pan.
4. Add the onion and brown slightly.
5. Crumble the meat into the frying pan and stir.
6. When the meat is brown, add the tomato mixture.
7. Turn the heat as low as possible. Simmer for 1 to 3 hours. The longer the sauce cooks the better it tastes. Stir occasionally. If the sauce gets too thick, add a little water.

The Spaghetti

1 eight-ounce box of your
favorite spaghetti

1. Fill a deep cooking pot with 2 quarts of water. Add 2 teaspoons of salt and bring to a rapid boil.
2. Break the spaghetti in half and slip it into the boiling water.
3. Add a few drops of vegetable oil to the water. This will keep the spaghetti from sticking together.
4. Turn heat to medium and stir spaghetti occasionally with a long-handled fork.
5. Cook for 8 to 10 minutes, until tender.
6. Have an adult pour the spaghetti and water into a colander placed in the sink.
7. Put the spaghetti on a large platter or in a large bowl, and spoon the sauce generously over the top.
8. Sprinkle with grated cheese or put the cheese shaker on the table.

Frankfurters with...
Cheese or Bacon

Frankfurters
Slices of cheese or strips of *cooked* bacon
Frankfurter rolls
1 tablespoon cooking oil

1. Cut the franks lengthwise, but don't cut through the skin on one side.
2. Heat a tablespoon of cooking oil in a frying pan. (Stove heat should be turned to medium.)
3. Lay the franks in the pan, flat side down.
4. Fry for about 2 minutes, then turn them over with a pancake turner.
5. Lay a strip of cheese over the franks, cover the pan, and let cook for another minute to melt the cheese.
6. If you prefer bacon, heat the cooked bacon in the uncovered pan and put on the franks before you serve them.

To Serve: Put the franks into warm frankfurter rolls, or serve them on a dinner plate with candied carrots (see page 42) and a mixed green salad (see page 41).

Frankfurters with...

Mustard, Relish, or Sauerkraut

1. Place a small saucepan of water on medium heat. Bring the water to a boil.
2. With a fork, poke several holes in each frank. This will keep them from bursting while they're boiling.
3. Slip the franks in the pot and cook for about 4 minutes.
4. When done, take out each frank with a long-handled fork, and put on a warmed plate.
5. Serve on warm frankfurter rolls with mustard or relish or sauerkraut.

For sauerkraut: Empty a small can of sauerkraut into a small pot. Warm over low heat while the franks are cooking. When ready to serve, lift by the forkful and let sauerkraut drain over pot before putting it on the frank.

In-a-Blanket

Tube of ready-to-bake crescent rolls

1. Heat the oven to 350°.
2. Wrap an unbaked crescent roll around each frankfurter.
3. Place the franks in a greased baking dish and bake for 13 to 15 minutes. Serve hot.

Baked Potatoes

Choose a medium-sized baking potato for each person. Choose potatoes that are all about the same size so that they will be done at the same time.

1. Heat the oven to 400°.
2. Wash and scrub the skins of the potatoes. Then dry them off.
3. Rub the skins with shortening or vegetable oil.
4. Prick each potato with a fork in about 4 places.
5. Set the potatoes on the oven rack without a pan.
6. Bake for 1 hour. Turn off oven.
7. Remove each potato, using a pot holder, and put it on a plate.
8. Cut a cross in each potato and tuck in a square of butter or margarine. Serve right away.

Note: If you are making baked potatoes to serve with meat loaf or baked chicken, put the potatoes in a hot oven (450°). After 15 minutes, turn oven to 350°, put in the meat loaf or chicken, and bake meat and potatoes for one hour at 350°.

Mixed Green Salad for Four

1 head of your favorite lettuce (iceberg, romaine, or Boston)

2 tomatoes
1 small cucumber

1. Separate the leaves of the lettuce and wash thoroughly. (Only wash as much lettuce as you will use. Store the rest in the refrigerator.)
2. Drain in a colander, then shake dry in a cloth towel.
3. Tear the lettuce leaves into small pieces.
4. Slice the tomatoes into about 6 pieces. Remove the stem ends.
5. Peel the cucumber and cut into thin slices.
6. Put the lettuce into a large bowl. Arrange the tomatoes and cucumber slices on top of the lettuce.
7. When ready to serve, add your favorite salad dressing and toss with a salad fork and spoon.

Candied Carrots

6 carrots
1 cup water
½ teaspoon salt
1 tablespoon butter or margarine

2 tablespoons brown sugar
water

1. Cut off the ends of the carrots. Scrape lengthwise with a parer and wash thoroughly.
2. Lay each carrot on a cutting board. Hold and cut in half lengthwise. (See Safety Tips 6 and 7, page 60.)
3. Lay each slice flat and cut again. Cut strips in half.
4. Put the cup of water into a medium-sized saucepan. Add the salt and bring to a boil.
5. Slip the carrots into the pot. Cook until tender when pricked with a fork — about 10 minutes.
6. Drain the carrots into a colander in the sink.
7. Put the butter, brown sugar, and 5 or 6 drops of water into a small frying pan. Stir over low heat until the butter, sugar, and water make a dark syrup.
8. Add the carrots and cook over low heat for 5 minutes. Turn the carrots with a fork so that they are coated all over.

Desserts and Party Treats

Chocolate Cupcakes

Makes 12 large cakes or 18 small ones

½ cup (1 stick) softened butter or margarine
1 cup granulated sugar
1 egg, beaten
½ cup sour milk
1½ cups all-purpose flour

½ cup cocoa
1 teaspoon baking powder
1 teaspoon baking soda
¼ teaspoon salt
¼ cup hot water
1 teaspoon vanilla extract

1. Heat the oven to 375°. Grease 12 cups of a muffin tin or line the cups with paper cupcake liners.
2. Make sour milk by adding 2 teaspoons of vinegar to ½ cup of whole, sweet milk.
3. Sift the flour, baking soda, baking powder, cocoa, and salt into a medium-sized bowl and mix well.
4. In a large bowl, mix the butter and sugar together with the back of a tablespoon until blended.
5. Add the beaten egg and stir until smooth.
6. Add some of the sour milk, then add some of the flour mixture to the egg mixture, a little at a time. Mix well after each addition.
7. When all the flour mixture and milk has been blended with the egg mixture, add the hot water and vanilla.

8. Mix thoroughly and beat until the batter is smooth.
9. Fill each muffin cup ⅔ full. Bake about 23 minutes. Let the cupcakes cool for 10 minutes before you remove them from the pan.
10. Serve plain or with ice cream. Or you can frost the cakes when thoroughly cooled.

   Note: For frosting, see next page.

Creamy White Frosting

2 tablespoons softened butter or margarine

3-oz. package of cream cheese

1 teaspoon vanilla extract

1¼ cups confectioners' sugar

Mix the softened butter, cream cheese, and vanilla in a medium-sized bowl until well-blended and creamy. Mix in the confectioners' sugar, adding a little at a time, and blend completely each time. Beat until mixture is creamy.

This will frost the tops of about 12 large cupcakes, or 18 small cupcakes.

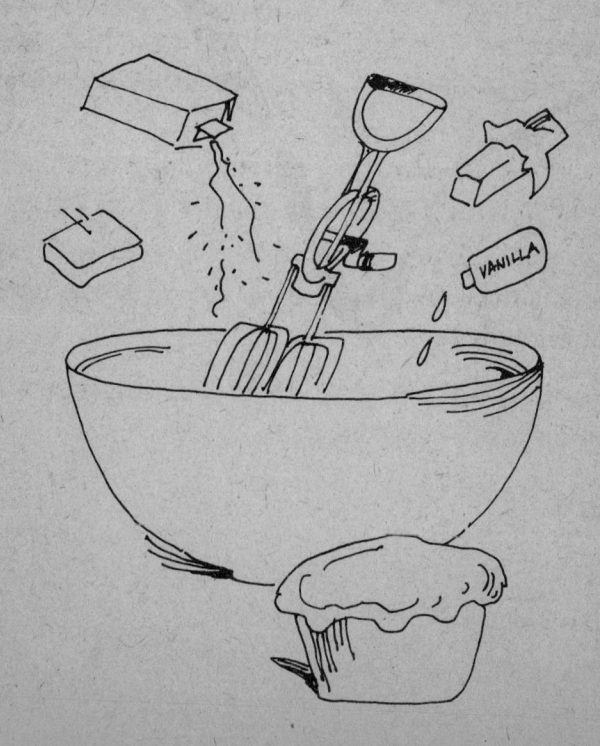

Ice Cream

Serves 6 people

 1 egg
¾ cup milk
½ cup heavy cream
¼ cup granulated sugar
dash of salt
⅛ teaspoon vanilla extract

1. Chill an 8-inch square baking pan in the freezer.
2. Break the egg into a bowl and beat well with an eggbeater.
3. Add the milk, cream, sugar, salt, and vanilla. Mix well with a spoon.
4. Pour into the chilled tray and put in the freezer. The ice cream will be firm in about 1 hour. You can serve it then, but it will taste even better if you beat it again and refreeze it.
5. To re-beat it, turn the ice cream into a chilled bowl and beat with a chilled eggbeater until fluffy.
6. Then quickly put it back into the chilled tray and return to the freezer. Leave undisturbed until it is firm enough to serve.

Serve plain or with apricot or strawberry jam, maple syrup, or chocolate sauce.

Refrigerator Cookies

You can use this recipe two ways: Keep the dough chilled in the refrigerator for days, and slice off refrigerator cookies whenever you want to bake; or bake regular drop cookies the same day you make the dough.

½ cup (1 stick) butter or margarine
1 cup granulated sugar
1 egg
1 teaspoon vanilla extract

1½ cups all-purpose flour
¼ teaspoon salt
1 teaspoon baking powder

1. Mix the butter and sugar together in a large bowl until creamy.
2. Beat the egg with a fork in a cup.
3. Add the egg and vanilla to the butter mixture. Mix well.
4. Sift the flour, salt, and baking powder together in another bowl.
5. Sift ⅓ of the flour mixture into the butter mixture and mix well.
6. Sift in another ⅓ of the flour mixture and mix well again.
7. Sift in the rest of the flour mixture and mix well.

If you want to make refrigerator cookies:
1. Shape the dough into a long roll—about 2 inches in diameter.
2. Wrap it in aluminum foil or plastic wrap.
3. Chill in the refrigerator for 12 to 24 hours, or longer.
4. When you are ready to bake, cut the cookies off the roll in very thin slices.
5. Put them on a greased cookie sheet.
6. Bake in a 400° oven for 8 to 10 minutes.

If you want to bake drop cookies right away:
1. Drop the batter by tablespoonfuls onto a greased cookie sheet.
2. Bake in a 400° oven for 8 to 10 minutes.

Chocolate Refrigerator Cookies

1. Melt 2 squares of unsweetened chocolate in the top of a double boiler over hot, but not boiling, water.
2. Add the melted chocolate to the cookie dough after all the flour mixture has been added.

Butterscotch Refrigerator Cookies

In making the cookie dough, use 1¼ cups brown sugar, well packed, instead of the 1 cup of white sugar.

Apple Crunch

5 or 6 baking apples
1 cup granulated sugar
1 cup all-purpose flour
⅓ cup butter or margarine
1 teaspoon baking powder
½ teaspoon salt
1 egg
cinnamon

1. Grease an 8-inch square baking pan.
2. Peel, core, and cut the apples into slices like orange sections. Arrange the apples in the baking pan.
3. Heat the oven to 350°.
4. Put the sugar, flour, baking powder, and salt in a bowl.
5. Break the egg into a cup, then add it to the sugar mixture.
6. Use a fork to mix it all together until crumbly.
7. Sprinkle the mixture over the apples.
8. Melt the butter or margarine in a small saucepan and pour it over the apples. Sprinkle cinnamon over the top.
9. Bake for 1 hour.
10. Serve hot or cold in dessert dishes with plain cream or with ice cream.

Apple Sauce

3 or 4 medium-sized, tart red apples
½ cup water
⅓ cup sugar
pinch of salt
2 pinches of cinnamon and/or slice of lemon

1. Wash, quarter, and core the apples.
2. Put them in a saucepan and add the water and salt.
3. Simmer over a low flame until apples are soft.
4. Remove from stove to sink. Put a colander in a large bowl and press the cooked apples through it with the back and edge of a large spoon.
5. Sift the sugar into the strained apples, mix, and taste. Add sugar as needed. Add cinnamon and/or lemon.

Note: If you prefer the cooked apples to have some shape, peel the quarters and slice them before you cook them. Add sugar, cinnamon, and/or lemon while they cook, and don't strain them.

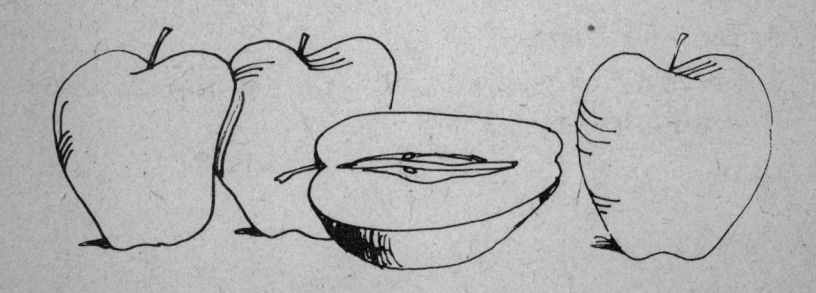

Chocolate Cookie Roll

Make this dessert about 4 hours before you want to serve it. Keep it in the refrigerator until you're ready to serve it.

20 thin chocolate cookies (you can use your own chocolate refrigerator cookies)

1 cup heavy cream
½ teaspoon vanilla extract
1 teaspoon granulated sugar

1. Chill a medium-sized bowl and an eggbeater in the refrigerator for about 15 minutes.
2. Whip the cream in the bowl, using the eggbeater.
3. Add the vanilla and sugar and continue beating until the cream is thick.
4. Spread the flat side of several cookies with a thin layer of whipped cream.
5. Stack the cookies, one on top of the other, then place them on edge on a long platter or large dish.
6. Continue spreading cream on the cookies and adding them to the roll on the platter.
7. When you have spread all the cookies, use the rest of the cream to cover the top and sides of the cookie roll.

To serve: When the roll is thoroughly chilled, cut slices at an angle. Makes about 8 ¾-inch slices of cake.

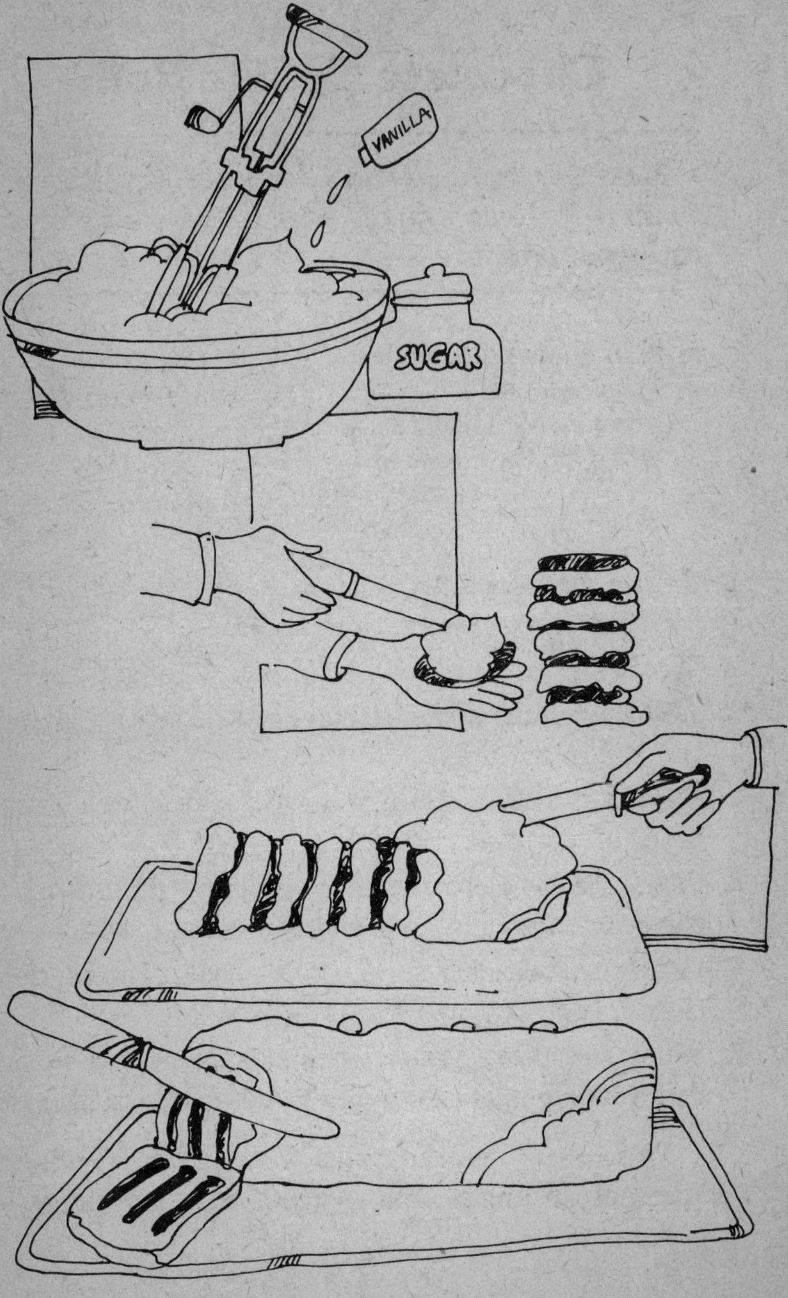
VANILLA
SUGAR

Cocoa

Makes 8 cups

½ cup cocoa
1 cup granulated sugar
½ cup milk

2 quarts milk or water, or a mixture of milk and water
½ tablespoon vanilla extract
8 marshmallows

1. Mix the cocoa, sugar, and the ½ cup of milk in a large saucepan.
2. Pour in the 2 quarts of milk or water—or the milk and water mixture. Stir.
3. Set the saucepan over low heat and stir constantly. Do not boil.
4. Remove from the heat.
5. Add the vanilla and stir.
6. Serve with a marshmallow floating in each cup.

Ribbon Sandwiches

4 thin slices of dark pumpernickel bread
3-ounce package cream cheese

1. Spread 3 slices of the dark bread, thickly, with cream cheese. Spread the cheese all the way to the edges.
2. Stack the slices, one on top of the other, so that you have a layer of bread, a layer of cheese, a layer of bread, etc. Top with a slice of plain pumpernickel bread.
3. Cut off the crusts.
4. Wrap in plastic wrap and put in the refrigerator for about 2 hours.
5. When you're ready to serve the sandwiches, cut the pile in 4 strips. You can cut each strip in half to make daintier sandwiches.

Makes 4 strips or 8 square sandwiches.

Make another pile of ribbon sandwiches using white bread and a dark filling—peanut butter or grape jelly. The trick is to use a dark filling with light bread and a light filling with dark bread.

Pinwheels

1. Use fresh, thin-sliced sandwich bread. Spread each slice with a layer of cream cheese. It can be tinted by mixing it in a bowl with a vegetable dye (green or yellow).
2. Or spread each slice with your favorite jelly or peanut butter, or both.
3. Trim off the crusts.
4. Roll up the bread—spread side in—and fasten with a toothpick.
5. Wrap in plastic wrap and put in the refrigerator for 2 hours.
6. When you're ready to serve, slice across the roll to make small pinwheels.

   For variety: Roll some of the slices corner to corner and leave uncut. Or use a cookie cutter to make different shapes for the colored cream cheese sandwiches. You can dot these with raisins, olive slices, or bits of green pepper or pimiento. No need to refrigerate the cut shapes.

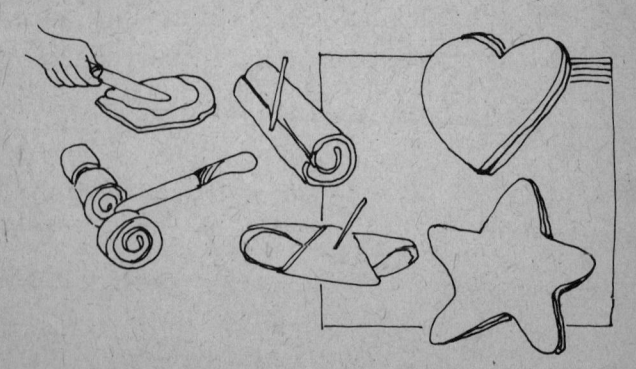

Celery Logs

4 or 5 stalks of celery
peanut butter and raisins

Wash and trim the celery. Cut into 4-inch pieces. Spread the inside of each stalk with peanut butter. Dot with raisins.

You can also fill the celery logs with a mixture of cream cheese and finely chopped olives or pickles.

Stuffed Eggs

1 hard-boiled egg per person
(see page 14)

1. Shell the eggs and slice each one in half, lengthwise.
2. Scoop the yolks into a bowl.
3. Add about 2 teaspoons of salad dressing for each egg.
4. Mash the yolks and salad dressing together.
5. Put the yolk back into the whites and dot with a stuffed green olive or a slice of sweet pickle.

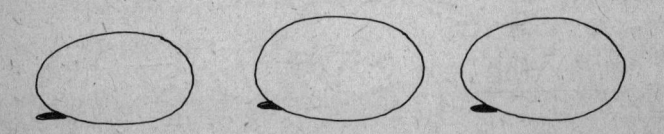

Lemonade

1 cup water
1 cup granulated sugar

1 cup fresh lemon juice (about 6 or 8 lemons)

1. Bring the water and sugar to a boil in a small saucepan.
2. Turn the heat low and simmer for 5 minutes.
3. Turn off the heat and stir in the lemon juice.
4. Empty a tray of ice cubes into a 2-quart pitcher.
5. Pour the lemon-sugar syrup over the cubes and fill the pitcher with cold water.
6. Put in the refrigerator until cold.

If you serve the lemonade in a punch bowl, double the recipe and add fresh fruit — lemon and orange slices and sliced strawberries — to float on top.

Sparkling Cranberry Punch

Makes 25 small cups

2 quarts chilled cranberry cocktail
1 can (6 ounces) frozen pink lemonade concentrate
1 quart ginger ale

Empty the cranberry cocktail and the frozen lemonade concentrate into a large punch bowl. Stir in the ginger ale. Make this just before you want to serve it so that it will be sparkling.

Pink Lemonade

If you would like to give your own lemonade an enticing, exotic pink color, you can do it by adding ¼ cup of cranberry cocktail or a tablespoon of grenadine syrup (it's non-alcoholic and made from currants), or with a little strawberry, cherry, or raspberry Jell-O.

To use Jell-O, put two level teaspoons of Jell-O powder in a cup. Add ¼ cup of boiling water and stir until thoroughly dissolved. Add ¼ cup of cold water and mix into your lemonade.

Safety Tips

1. If you have long hair, tie it back out of the way.
2. Don't wear long beads, ties, or loose sleeves that could catch on pot handles and tip them over.
3. Have an adult present when you're cooking—to turn on the oven or stove, to help lift heavy or very hot pots and pans, and help you test the food.
4. Use pot holders when you lift pots off the stove or take pans or baked potatoes out of the oven.
5. Turn handles of pots sideways so that they don't stick out past the edge of the stove, where they could catch or be bumped, and tip over. Touch handles lightly before grabbing them. They can get hot!
6. Use a cutting board when you're chopping vegetables. Put the vegetables flat on the board and cut down, away from your fingers. Cut all rounded vegetables in half, then lay the flat side on the board before chopping. Skin onions before cutting.
7. Use small paring knife to cut vegetables, and a parer to scrape a carrot or potato.
8. You don't have to use electric juicers, mixers, blenders or can openers for any of the recipes in this book. If you do use them, ask an adult to help.

Cooking Tips

1. Wash and dry your hands before you start to cook.
2. Wash all fresh vegetables and fruits.
3. Wear an apron to protect your clothes.
4. Get all the ingredients you will use before you start making a recipe. Once you've used an ingredient, put it to one side — so you'll know you've used it.
5. Measure ingredients exactly. Level off measuring spoons or measuring cups with the back of a knife. Scrape the knife across the top of the spoon or cup. (Three teaspoons equal a tablespoon. Four tablespoons equal ¼ cup.)
6. Cream sugar and butter together by rubbing them against the side of a bowl with the back of a spoon until they are smooth and soft.
7. Grease baking pans and dishes with a small piece of waxed paper dipped in softened butter or margarine.
8. Test cupcakes for doneness by sticking a toothpick into the center. If the toothpick comes out dry, the cupcakes are done.
9. Let bread and cupcakes cool in the pan about 10 minutes before you place them on a cake rack. Do not put icing on cakes until they are completely cool.

Cooking Equipment